Does Someone

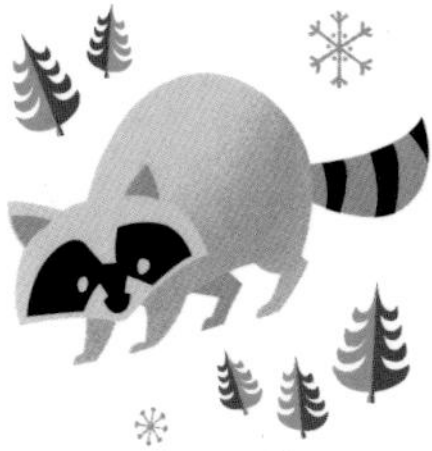

Does Someone

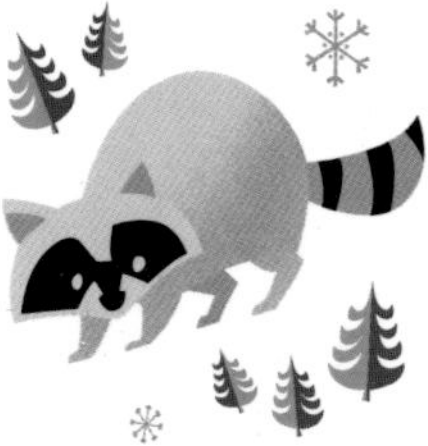

Need a Hug?

LEFT SIDE

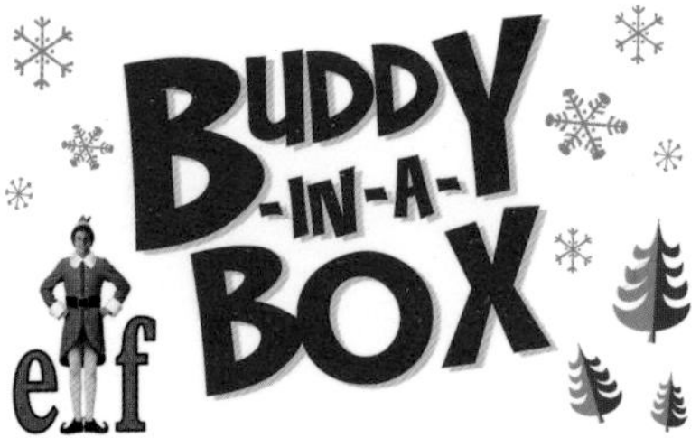

TOP

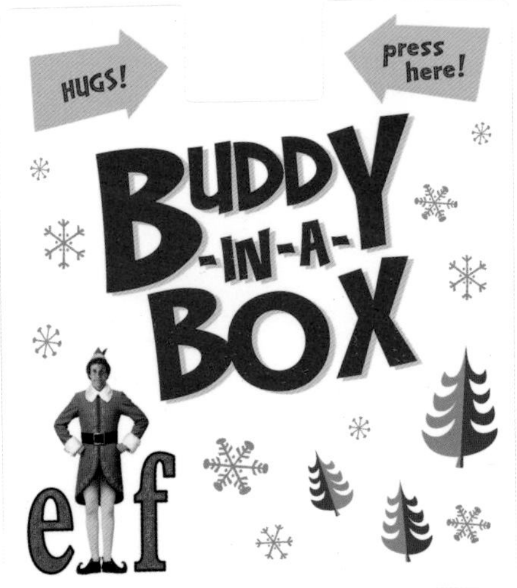
HUGS!
press here!
BUDDY -IN-A- BOX
elf

FRONT

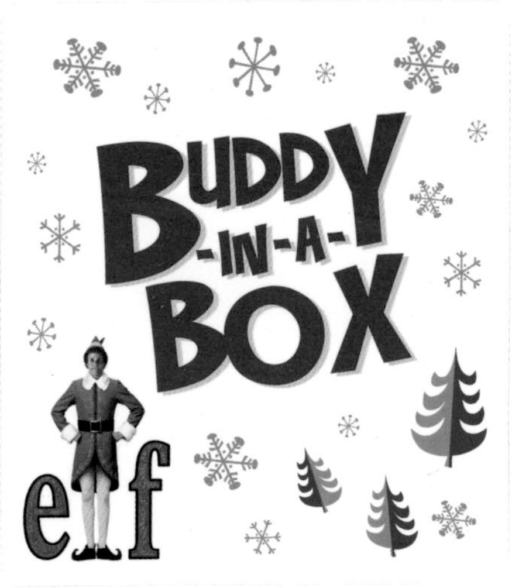

BACK